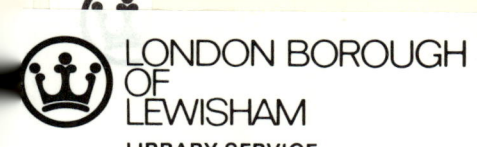

THE VENUS TOUCH

500 copies of a limited edition of this book
have been published, each numbered and signed
by the author, of which this is number 3 7 7

The Venus Touch

Poems by
MAUREEN DUFFY

WEIDENFELD AND NICOLSON
5 Winsley Street London W1

Some of these poems appeared originally in *Contact*
Magazine.

The drawings by Egon Schiele and Gustav Klimt are
reproduced by kind permission of the Courtald
Institute, Marlborough Fine Art Ltd., and Jean-Jacques
Pauvert.

Printed in Great Britain by
Lewis Reprints Limited, London

CONTENTS

☬ Snowtime

I make for you in snowtime a poem
Simple as the figures children build,
Father or lover, with upturned smiling mouth
And the gleam of faceted eyes,
To stand beyond your window after dark
Among the arrow prints of birds
And the hung fleece of leaves,
The moulded lines firm and strong,
For the child in you to clap hands,
Lead me wondering into the garden;
And I make it out of the white drift of love.

Oh Penelope, what did you do?
Slip a corn dolly between the sheets
In likeness of a man?
Straw coloured hair, o fair
Achaen, and the eyes you might have made
Of some island speedwell.
Did you talk to it as you loomed
A warp of a life, were you faithful
To its unanswering fixed stare
That might have been anyone's,
The clamourers in the courtyard,
Jove come down, a passing pedlar
With ballads of his own pain?

I wouldn't have blamed you.
Times among the flat fields
I lost your face. I knew I loved
And your name but it had
No lineaments and that was Persephone's
Hour who never wanted me till I had you
Then took all shapes to lead me from my course.
I am come home but the shutters are down
In that house, all asleep
While the beggar lingers outside
Nursing his scar, the wound of love
You branded into his flesh.

Let me walk in your dreams
And tomorrow again I will draw
My bow at your venture, run up
Your steps and drive our shadows
Mewling into the dark.

Tutto Tremante

Thinking on three who trembled:
Sappho alone at midnight pale as winter grass,
The roseboy struck to the bone with chill ever after,
Paolo betrayed by imagination, wordspell,
And her mouth, her mouth,
I question if their thighs ached as mine do,
Their breath clotted so thick in the throat,
Desire flushed like gall in the gut
Still after this time passed
When we cling crying to each other,
Die, resurrect to die again; still, still,
After a day's tombed eternity,
I am all trembling for you.

Should I wear masks for you?
Should I counterfeit and strut on the stage of myself,
Suspend your disbelief with play?

I am all lovers; in me their lines meet
Or in your infinity who are all queens
Divinely right. So we lift them
From the flat page, endow with shape and colour
And the dimension of love;
Make of their temporal our long present,
Rehearse, repeat the gestures, phrases
Compounded of lust and tenderness.
Only do not look at me like that
Or I forget my words.

Stand with me now at the death of the year
Where we first loved.
Though they lay pennies on its eyes,
Wind it with oblivion and earth it deep
The grave figures are hatched on our hearts
And start green from the soil
With every day's new Spring.

Say again we have built an empire,
That our white sphere outlives mere kingdoms;
For immortality. Lay all seige to us
Our walls are battlemented,
No little wicked gate lets out a traitor
Since we are citizens and emperors
That rule tenderly in each other's weal.

I am love's fool, clown for you,
Divert your days, antic and stumbling;
Tumble the bauble my heart
For your delight. If you smile
I am rewarded, paid in your pleasure,
The soft cries that bring me down
Hawk to your trembling.

You, love's garner, hold our harvest
In your arms. Our joy runs in your mild flesh
Warm as milk, nurturing us both.
Spent I rock in the bay of belly and breasts,
Am gathered and held while you kiss me to life
Til I am sword again, the devourer
Who would eat your heart.

Let this duality swing between us,
Our sacrament, giving and given.
Be my autumn, I your fierce summer;
My winter dying you wake to Spring.
So we shall turn and turn on love
As easy as blending months or the to and fro of tides
And never go lonely into new year again.

Stand with me then. They are tolling for us
A death and a birth who are ever
Dying and reborn, who are bound
Out of time and all passing.
Give me your hand. We will write on this stone
In letters heart deep that all may know
Marvelling how we love.

◎ Tzarskoë Selo

Not that I love you more when snow falls;
That would be to make the heart seasonal,
Determined by time and place,
Yet you are my winter palace
Of agate and marble,
And I wonder in your rooms,

Cap in hand, that the guards should let me in,
Take my dull coins as currency,
Allow my muddy boots to track
The fretted floors;
Let me finger the damask bed-hangings,
Baldacchinoed high altar where we perform our rites
Stare unwashed into the bath-house,
Leave breadcrumbs among the silver
And blackprint the courtyard's purity;
Inherit riches my tongue stumbles over
Like a child at a party with too much cake
Who cannot say thankyou and, 'I like it.'

Always you surprise me, mouth agape,
In some far chamber where the public are forbidden
Happen upon me, winter queen jewelled and reigning
When I have nothing to offer but homage
And the snowball in my hand.

⊗ Legends

One   Cherubino

Knowing he loved her more than children should
They packed him off to fight;
The foreign wars would make a man of him.
That steel severance took him in the heart.
They brought him girls and mocked him
To be brave. Perhaps he wrote
From his billet in the town,
'Madam, I commend...' and wept,
And drank; the cherub lad become a soldier shell.
No history tells us
How the blank days failed for her.

Made man they sent him back. Masked
He enters the swaying hall,
Searches the dancers for remembered eyes,
A gesture. Leads her willingly away.
Remembering she cries on love.
Her voice, echoing in the sac that held his heart,
Provokes to lust. Beyond the long windows,
In the glittering garden, the marble death
Stirs to embrace them both.

Two   Guenever

Six weeks he lingered, shrunk on salt tears
And fasting two span from that first height
That would have overtopped the world
For her. They laid him in her bier
To bury him. That final parting:
All day she walked knowing he would be there
Suddenly, lifting her eyes swooned and then,
Her last bitch trick he saw through,

15

Loved her for: 'Have bliss of someone else.
You never will keep faith.'
But dared not kiss him
And dying prayed two days never to see
His face again since that flame,
That envy fanned to war, leapt in her still.

So he went away bound her captive,
Glad in his chains as he had always been.
And the sweet fragrance his body held
That we hanker after, reading between the lines,
Know it the distillation of their love.

⊖

Between you and me
Lie the childhood images
Playing out mothers and fathers
Patterns of loving
On a wet afternoon.

Between you and I
Two egos stand
Defying the grammar of the heart
In tactical attitudes
Pretentiously incorrect.

Between us
There is nothing but love
An indivisible object
Where both are subject
Entwined without accusation.

Between there is nothing but love.

⊘ Allegory

Frail child you wept yourself to sleep,
The silk string snapped.
Carnivorous, cloven footed
The centaurs rage through arcady;
Lovers and poets cower among the rocks:
Strumpetted, assailed the goddess swoons,
Thrust back by the coarse hands, blackly overhung;
Her sweet flesh vulture prey,
Mere carrion. Adonis gored bleeds into the dust.

Accept this litany. By all the live dead
Who held in word or line
The flimsy barricade against that tyranny,
Opposed with their quick breath
The oligarch destruction and dying,
Shot down in the public square,
Among debris of torn tissue
Delicate as insect wing,
Proclaimed and yet we live;
Over whom we raise slight temples
Of our longing and faith
Intangible as moonlight,
By these presents I conjure you
Grow strong, winged again.

You have taught us your songs,
Pierced us til we bleed ambrosia.
Rarefied among your stars we cannot live
On the weighted earth where the days die
Anonymous, unmarked.

Listen, I wake you; mend up your bow.
We wipe your tears. Sleeping a little,
You dreamed we walked hand in hand
Through smiles among the painted sunlight
While nymphs crept out of the trees.
It shall be so.

◯ Habits

You didn't turn at the door:
A habit broken that might have impaled us
On repetition, that not turning
I might think, 'What did she mean?'
Or the act become a formality
When none can muffle the sound
Of tearing flesh.
So we break habits deliberately
Like priceless vases dropped
On a concrete floor to show
We can stand the shock, have courage
To take the symbol and throw it away.

Yet there are habits less easily fractured.
The habit of being without you
Once broken doesn't mend so soon;
I plug the gap with drink and talk
Yet every echo uncovers the void
That is always there, that I hide,
Camouflage with light and shade of gossip
Lest stumbling you glimpse the depths
That house me apart and take fright.

Torn I tack it together; a botched job
Cobbled up with cat's teeth but it will do
Unless you should break that habit of loving me,
The seams tear open and I tumble headlong into
                                    dark.

You sleep now, my self in your arms.
My weight lies smooth, heavy
Between your breasts and thighs.
Homeless my thoughts wander the city,
Walk the waters of Thames,
Light as others' dreams.

Feel that quick touch?
That was my mouth on yours.

Ghost, unfleshed since you hold my substance
I am all air and fire;
All water too, liquefy in tears
Like classic heroes who wept unshamed
At love or fate.

'Why out so late?' They stop me
In the street, shine torches in my eyes.
Revenant, unhoused I stammer blind.
'No fixed abode?' Their notebooks poise.
Tell them I have a lodging close at hand;
Surety, bond; that doors stand wide for me
And, with daylight, you will take me in.

Last night, oh last night
I was Antony, emperor.
Tonight the climbing boy creeps snivelling
To his sack in the corner
And there is no coverlet flesh
To keep out the draughts.

 'Nessun maggior dolore,'

They remembering that bliss they missed,
When the age was golden,
Rose daily along the pathways of smiles,
Was harnessed to thundering light,
Called that the greatest pain
Yet endured and love never left them.
Still they wandered hell together
Though pared to shades
As I would do always
That we might not be divided.

But now let us take back our sun.

It is as though, swopping remembrances
Many coloured as a bag of marbles,
Songs and comics, we had been
Children together yet I know
We would never have met.
Ranging the backchats I was some
Wild creature you weren't allowed to play with,
Hunted with the rough pack,
Hallooing like Tarzan into the dusk
And didn't wear socks.
Did you ever, I wonder, look out
Beyond your driveway where the swart shapes
Capered under the lamp? Does your compassion
For dumb beasts date from this time?

Even then I loved you. Knew before
You showed me the turretted house,
On an afternoon of windy visitation
When the streets were torn open with winter,
I drank tea, you coffee
Reminding us we would never have met,
That you were the Rapunzel I imaged
When the gang had gone home to bed
And I was left scuffing my boots
Alone, looking in through lit windows
Where the angel fish trailed their lace doyleys
In the bought sunlight of their tropical tank.
You were imprisoned, I knew,
Or else you would come out and play
And I should rescue you but you must
Let down your hair for me to climb up.
No one would say which window held you.

Later we might have met learning
But again I could have loved you
Only in the distance, written you poems,
Followed you home dawdling well back,
The immutable class laws of children,
'She's in the Upper Fifth, you're only in Lower
                                            Four,'
Keeping us apart still.

So I have pursued you impossibly
Under all guises, dragging behind
Til last you turned and let me catch up;
Let fall that ladder to mount,
Possess your castle. It's good
To be grown up. 'Now no one
Can stop us playing together.'
Our games are more innocent than children's.

Tell me a story.
Let there be dragons and ogres
For I am used to them;
A unicorn who gave himself up for a lady,
Horned in on captivity,
And shot his bolt.
But let it be alright
In the end.

Tell me a story
While we lie embedded in each other's arms,
My mouth in your hair
So I hold my breath with listening
And the words fall, sonorous caresses,
On my head. The Spring afternoon
Draws mild curtains across our windows
Of woven rain and sunwarp.

Tell me your story
And I will weep or laugh.
The syllables spell us a charm for healing,
Bind our sore places with webs
And moonshine, exorcise.
Bereaved children we follow
Each other's wanderings.
There was once a princess...

The woodcutter loved her.
Such tales are true.

one

Her shuddering angel scattering light like sperm,
Air upborne with goldtipped arrow poised,
Whose smiles beat down her shuttered eyes,
Engenders ecstasy; subject she lies
Bound with her heart strings
While the molten tides flush through her thighs.
Lips part to let those cries
Break in prayers, not sighs.

How can her seraph,
Dazed with her rending softness,
Whose mouth has sucked the salt weep
Of her wound that dart provokes, like milk,
Play again among cherubs,
Children; announce to virgins
The triumph of harrowing flame?

two

Some darksoul nights her seraph does not come.
'Crucified between heaven and earth,'
Limbo held she waits
His resurrection.
Fallen, hell-bent, he droops.
Those pinions lank with tears
Cannot vault him
Over the walls of light.
Dull iron blunts his spear.
The bloodied shadows dance across his eyes
Mocking that bliss, that breast,
Her ecstasy he made his own.
Lured by their joy he hammers at her door
Plunging the crude shaft
Again, again into her flesh;
Her moans, not rapture but sharp pain,

Drive off their heaven
And hurl him Icarus down
Who dared the sun.

Become her torment dark angel
Beats back the soft arms
That would catch him close,
Hold him serene in that white drift
Where he might lay his mouth,
Suck peace sweet as milk;
His pain a lash fiercer
Than any whip until she falls trembling.
Her last breath, his kiss to life
She gives him out of love,
Stirs the bedraggled plumes,
Rising he puts on light,
Invests them in his rays.
Fire-tipped she takes him swooning to herself,
Brided, broken, giving, given,
And who shall tell their ecstasy apart?

✪ *Der Rosenkavalier*

one

The footmen are in league
So do not trust them.
Malice or sloth cancel out your wage.
A barbershop quartet they watched him through
                                    the window,
Ready with soft soap or the knife,
And tittered while he pressed
His forehead to the horse's flank,
Seeing the road scurry under the hooves,
The years of Sunday roasts,
The lusts in three-four time;

Prayed she would call him back
Then rode away unarmed.

Your fears report you lonely.
Do not believe them.
In our play all roles are doubled:
It is also you I bring the silver rose.

two

Tonight he sleeps away. She rises
To stop the clocks and hold up time;
No pause for the gilt and wanton loves
That smile their chiding. The hand
Trembles over the inexorable faces.
Tomorrow at her toilet she will pluck
A silver hair and shrink from the wizened
Sadness of the pet ape. Her lover hunts her
Through the corridors of years. Poor ghost,
She flits from room to room in the small hours,
Insubstantial as chiffon
Crying, 'You can never catch me.'

Stand still. Turn to face him.
He too grows old in your footsteps,
Dragging your despair. Submit to love.
In all dying our ages are the same.

three

Imp you first attend the lady,
Bring her breakfast, restoratives
After a night of love,
Make straight, lay out her mask
While he skulks behind the bedcurtains,

Trailing his sword.
Bearer of love, go-between,
She sends you with his last commission,
Dismissed. Only in the last act
She would have you follow her still
But you are alone on stage
And dance away with a wisp of handkerchief.

Let her look for a new servant;
She will not find one so brisk, so meet
To her command. That other child,
Paleface, languorous will usurp your place.

four

He was proud being young,
Took his hurt out into the street
And rode away. He was wrong
Being young. Did he think
She might send after him, call him
Back, or feel God and custom
A windmill he could not tilt?
His wound bled slow. Dried blood
Feeds roses. Three times he calls her,
'Marie Thérèse,' an invocation that
Cannot bring her close. He stands between,
Equidistant in the trio while she soars.
I learn from him. No pride shall spur me
Out of sight. I will not leave that room:
The casket cannot hold my petalled heart.
I am too old to play she loves me not.

☯ *Eurydice II*

Dead hands jealous some days drew her back.
Gathering flowers she stooped;
Earth opened, that chariot stood ready,
Funereal horses tossed their hearse black plumes,
Mutely the dark king beckoned
Her sullen feet.

In the empty house he hears
The hush in the garden,
The song her heart sang towards him stilled,
Runs from the room hurling his frantic notes
Into the air to stay that flight.
Fiercely he holds her; the earth closes.

Yet if it were all to do again:
Charon, Cerberus, the manyheaded dead,
He would take his terror and his pocketful
Of rhymes, fling down the scraps of love
To fill that maw; bribe, busk or plead
And drive her stumbling up towards the sun.

☯ *Limbo*

In Limboland they wait
Who are neither living nor dead
But beyond grace;
For whom eternity passes without presence.
So I inhabit for a time this negative,
Knowing that you too are walking apart
Among your dead,
Until my saint summon me
With your speaking eyes
And I put on redemption
With your flesh.

☯ *Epistle*

Once
There was a time,
The calendar tells me,
When we were not,
When this so present was future
And the past a range
Of crooked queries marking off the years.
Call it the dreamtime
For there was nothing about it of Eden;
Was aboriginal, mist-shaped,
Myself someone who never dreamed in colour.
Since my birth I hardly remember it
Except when its fears overtake me
Alone, afraid of the dark, and I scurry
To placate those malign spirits
With gravings of your name
On rocks and pictures of lovers
Done in my own blood.
Sometimes then I thought I glimpsed you
But it was only the mirage of my own desire
Dancing away over the naked plain
And withdrew to vanishing point
When I tried to come close.
Today, our birthday, I would not
Burden with hung symbols
When all are feastdays, holydays
But to say look at me love
With those eyes that starred our nativity
Only clearer by a year.
They show me all the colours of loving
And all my life is present on your breast.

When I was young I used to sleep
On the bare ground, spreadeagled
In the sun, my face against the coarse grass hair,
Imagining the ooze of tiredness
Seep down from my pores through fibres, topsoil,
Slither over the unwilling clay to be sopped up
At last by the indifferent compassion of chalk.

Now, my cheek bedded soft in your hair,
I straddle your warm earth,
Know the ache in the heart's bones
Eased by your arms; the rise
And fall of your breath surf soothe
All abrasions and the scrutiny of your love
Hold me safefast while I sleep.

Let fall from love you take
Such postures as Titian,
Correggio, Giorgione
Stroked for Danäe, Antiope,
Venus; seeded by gold shower,
Satyrized sleeping, fucked drowsy
An arm under her head
As white roses heavy with bees'
Predations droop blowsed petals,
Lambent under the full lips of the sun;
Display their pistil wounds
Where bruising tongues
Filched honey while they smiled.
Generous of yourself you offer
Curving perspectives, limbs sagged under love,
To progress with eyes, hands, mouth
While you lie open, falling as   31
Water, sunlight, petals.

⊛

That running upstairs child you deprecate,
Would banish back down your years,
Cries to me sometimes, 'Lost!'
From the vertigo of dreams.
'That door, was it left or right?
Where was time while I bent my head
Over the album, the coloured names
Carrying me away?' I stretch a hand,
Knowing the least hair's fall,
To that child loved always for the woman
Who last night cried wild in my arms,
Swept beyond yourself and running
Up stair and stair to joy.

⊛

Picture's end. Across the split mouth of the screen
Hero and heroine, stumbling a little
Under the burden of our hope, run,
Arms spread to catch up our hearts
And hold them between rehearsed lips.
In the moist wombdark where others sit alone
With their dreams I clench your hand
Whose warmsilk contours I have kneaded,
Traced the cuticle ridges, stabbed myself
To pain pleasure on the cat point nails,
Stuck fast in our sweated balm,
Through their reeling saga of lost and found.
The lights spot out the unshamed glitter
On my cheeks. All hours away
I run towards you with my burden hope,
Arms stretched on emptiness,
Air slipstreaming through my hollow bones,
To consummation on your mouth
And our saga's beginning.

There is no balm. The time apart
Bleeds slow and thick still
And will not be sutured
With tendrils of music,
Bound with soft words remembered.
You walk away in my head,
Scuff up my quick loss
As children's uncaring shoes
The leaves of our second autumn,
Crossing the road head up
So you may not see the damply clinging shapes
That would clog your feet.

The labyrinth hours tunnel ahead
Through which I follow the unwinding of
The lover's knot my saint
Placed in my hands to guide me
While the minotaur bellows in my dark.
Yet he shall not have me.
Legend is on my side.
Bedded in our enchanted island,
Myself, the fierce god, shall comfort you,
Roaring through your dark,
For all desertions.

The poor sod in the next cell
Is breaking up his bed.
I hear his tears and rage,
The impotent grief
Of a wild thing new trapped.
'Can't do his bird,'
The screw grins through portcullis teeth.

Before he was limed
His bird down in his arms
Beat against his caging ribs,
Fluttering her cries soft into his mouth
As he stroked her dying,
A canary set in the sun.

'Can't do his bird.'
Should be patient,
Take it like a man.
I hammer warder on his door,
'Shut up in there.'

'Oh my dove, my heart,'
I hear him weep and
The voice is my own,
Not even the thickness of skin between us,
These my hands abraded on the unanswering stone.

⊗

Though you hide under mountains
The same pain torments us.
I know when you wince
By the contraction of my heart.

⊗

Shisaku in snow:
I press up into your ice
Lake and you fall on
Me in white flakes. Hot love words.

⊗

You shall not ever, my love,
Be left to wander lost
Down that white dream road.
I am the scarecrow at
Your furthest vision
Who holds out arms to bar
And hold you. I am
The feet running behind
That will not let you stray.
Daedelus on my strong wings
I bear us home while you are couched
Warm among my plumes,
Your cheek laid to my neck.
Soon I shall lead you again
To the eternity of our bed.
I will never let you go.

⊗ *Sleep*

Twin brother to death you have
His looks, hooded, featureless,
'Before me,' you say, 'all men are passive,
Fall back under my weight
Heavy lidding their eyes, sink.
Why should you strive against me?'

Beast you take her from me,
Ravish her into dreams
Where I cannot Perseus hover
Putting out dragons nor even an arm
To hold her when she weeps
Naked to demons under your spell.

You part us daily. Leave me
Adrift in Acheron doubting if daylight
Will ferry me back to life.
Curtains shrouding the window
Are blazoned with dogs' heads
That would keep me from crossing that river

Oh sweet sour Thames where my love
Might glide in apotheosis of sunrise,
Blood and gold. I take against you
These words. After three days sleepless
Men die. I toss and turn
And will not let you in.

Or if I do start waking
In that prime hour of lovers, mystics,
Small animals who seek their heart,
Their hunger in your despite,
Weeping alone in their narrow beds,
Burrows, small salt pearls
That may, like this, be any price.

☮ Triptych

And out of this unspilt seed,
Those that cannot be mine
Bourne in your billowing sail
My piracy stormed,
I offer you pearls, tears
You will not shed
For that daughter I love
In your belly or the cradle of your arms,
Knowing you must let her go
To other lovers like me.

I with neither past nor future
But only your present
Frescoed day by day,
Blocking in our design,
Stretch to you, aureoled for me
In that descending order
Midway in the triptych
Mothers and daughters,
Purgatoria, my saint, madonna,
Hands that would soothe
Your past and future into our present
Canopying you with my love
Through the long night apart.

✡ *Graphics for St Valentine*

ice crystals etch your
name on this glass to erase
it splinter my heart.

love all devourer
wolfs music image word yet
hungers for your flesh.

sucking to the rind
each minute of you honeyed
fruit I waste for more.

heavy eyed we sit
unwilling that night should rear
itself between us.

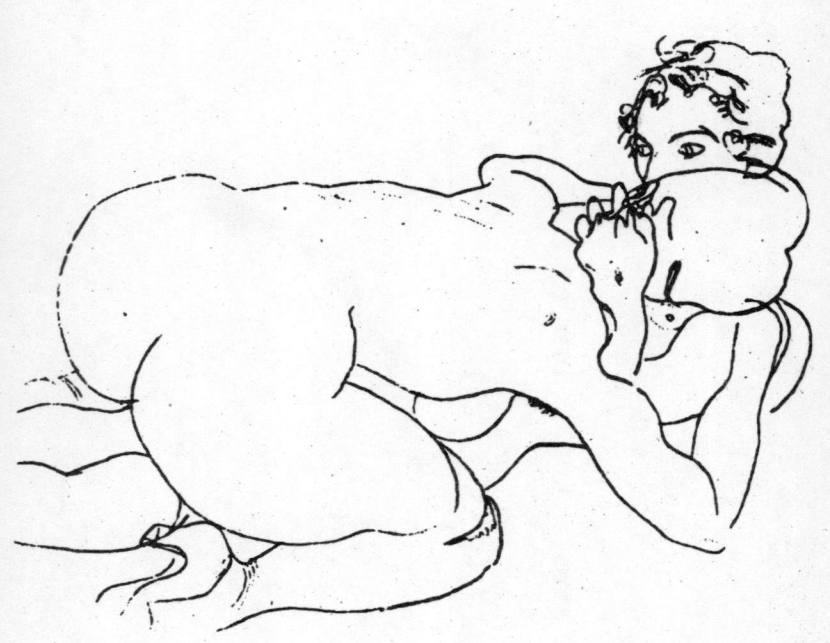

✡ *Logically from John Donne*

Driving away from you is
Always to be night
Driving East into setting
Sun under branches
Black between waters through park
Where last night you said,
'O beautiful it is this
City and our love.'
No, not twilight. Full dark falls
Numbing as thunder
Clap at once tropical and
Arctic so that this
Paradox of driving East
Into day's fall is
Heart's syllogism; this end
Inherent in that
Premise: we love, and to be
Absent is to be
Gone West, benighted; homing
Is into sunrise
By ratiocination
Of blood since you are
Lodestar, compass. I would drive
Our sun's chrome bright car
In reverse with wild horse power,
My desires, til I brake
Stand shuddering at your door.

I recognise this landscape,
Have inhabited these dead surfaces
For no one lives here,
All are travellers passing through
Or guests merely in some bleak
Boarding house where time is transfixed,
Doors and casements keyhole on blackness,
A comb, alien and titan, usurps the bed.
Home is always elsewhere
Guilt haunted; the ideal,
Cotton wool clouds on baby blue,
Is the eye's false image;
Reality and art confound in the canvas pane
Both irrelevant. Only wit
Sees us through: a golden manna
Of French bread.

I have leant on the parapet
Of a dawn bridge, blackwinged,
Or walked my corpse at night
By beckoning water; gone towards pleasure
While myself turned away.
Today revoking that past
In the detritus of living, bills, letters
Beaucoup de souvenirs, I scented
Terror: that drowned cadaver
Would clasp and drag me under.
But it was another, an old country.
In this land where you walk with me
Light echoes from planes textured
Soft as your mouth, vibrates in
The laughter of kisses, is
Oh alive.

✡ Lines to go with a Lily

Yellow trumpets
Annunciate the year's resurrection
From every corner barrow
And I poise
Letting love fall about me
Like sunlight
On the threshold of our third summer
Telling you drop the chaste ice chains
Winter links about your heart,
Open to the knock
Of this stave
Tender yet obstinate
As daffodils
And bear our joy, my pride,
Before you
Swelling with our Spring.

Wishing to erect for you
In grave lines some headstone
Cusped with cupidons,
And heads-I-win with
Bifronting Janus
As children build castles
Crying, 'Come see before the waves
Lay down our mortality,
Our aspiration on the pebbled shore,'
Some prompter to rehearse
Our two-year sovereignty
For your applause,

I stub bare feet on the knowledge
That for you time runs
Neither backwards nor forwards;
Is instant now. I watch you
Building in this sunlight,
Sculpting from golden fragments,
And lug my marker far out
Across the puddled sand
To where the tide lies back.
See, those amoretti are heaping
Our seawall, laughing in the ripples.
You can play here safe til nightfall.

⊗ *Aria for Midsummer's Eve*

Extol me her midsummer flesh,
Lay your praises over the wounds of absence,
Poultice of dew heavy leaves from the dream wood;
Wordspell solace.

All charms are hers. On this eve
Arias sing about her; there is wine
And strawberries by the water where queen
She leans and smiles.

Alone I wrench time and layer
Days and nights, sweet and sour, in my angel cake
Of loving since our clock has no hands,
Ours is ever,

And our occasions hang gauzing
Each other; this year last though absent I
Page beside you over the lawns, pin up
Froth of hedge lace

The white folds at your breast I traced,
Limning its silk swags' moondrawn swell as if
You lay pregnant with our high summer love,
Last night abed,

Span your belly with a warming hand
Yet double vision you driving home under
A night sieved with stars or late plucking for me
Dogrose kisses.

☿

I am beset with a dream of fair woman,
Lunatic for Venus flesh
So sweet in the night
I do not know if I have woven her,
Pygmalion, out of my desires
Or if indeed those hours she lay
Beside, under me.
Happy the hand that touches her,
The cloth that drapes her,
The eyes and words that catch hers.
Where she is the skies are
Clouded with loves, the minutes dove drawn.
I whimper in this waking sleep
Remembering as dogs run down past quarry,
Hunter and snared by my dream of fair woman,
Lunatic for your Venus flesh.

♁ *Haikus*

Starved a week for your
Body I glut on glimpsed sweets
Your breast between folds.

If you would leave me
Be as we are with old dogs
Kind, sweet kill me first.

Daphnis and Chloe
Apart at night wept. Their dawn
Rose faster than mine.

⊗

Bastard siblings I
Father on absence that trull
I suffer when she, joy,
Is away, my poems,
When we look babies,
My eyes plunged in hers,
We make strong children
Of laughter that run off
Nimble as our time
Together with no
Need of nursery rhymes
To rock their puling.

⊗

Bed whose sheets she chose
Tiepoloed with sunrise,
My aurora, where two nights
I lay in cloudy bliss, hero's hand
Shielding her breast, limbs lapping
Hers as the rough calyx
The wantonness of silk corolla,
Tonight I stretch my arms
Through your wastes become
Unyielding as pink marble,
Verona's paving stones in chill dawn,
Capulet's tomb, and hanker
For that other hard narrow cot
Where we lovered
Short hours till she slept,
Her breath coming and going
On my cheek as Eros fanned
Venus and Mars, murmuring me,
Her face child smoothed by my lips,
Cupid's kisses, scented as violet
Cachous as I watchdogged her dreams.
Bed, tonight you are too wide;
Your pillowy flesh no comfort.
My bones ache and toss in your chaste unease.

⊗ A Litany for St Venus del Parto, Monterchi

My lady of the bursting belly
Split like a ripe fruit,
Chestnut, tomato,
In this poured gold morning
As if all autumn were your
Gathered festival,
The palanquin held open before you,
Figured with maidenhair tendrils,
Is the lips of your own sweet part
O where I Gabriel
Fucked you with a lily
That you may scatter light seeds,
My fecund goddess,
Venus genetrix,
In men's minds.

No wonder if the dead lie at your feet;
Do we not blazon
Tombs with cupids in
Token of resurrection,
Knowing that only love can
Put out death? Black
Cypresses brushing their cameos on
The horizon are everlasting,
Shed no gilt poplar patina.
Let the dead bury the dead.
Calmly your hand unpicks a seam
Like Caesar's or a ripped pea
Pod that you may dream
Virgin unbroken,
Ma donna.

You cannot fool me with your simple
Blue dress cut elegant
As a queen's (an old trick
Madam, and this veil over
My eyes so that the day aches
With you and brilliance)
Nor the peasant women wanting lovers
Who have brought you oblations
To this fane longer than your picture
Has reigned serene in its white shrine;
You are only a girl, a child
Even sometimes in my arms,
Yet I know you too,
Goddess, whore, mother,
And adore you.

⊗ Chinoiseries

1. Autumn

Sparrows and leaves fall in the garden,
Burnt paper of birds, bronze foil
Of foliage, dying year's tokens.

If I were stout, rich with empire's spoils
I would build you a pavilion
Whose walls, like in the story, rang with bells.

And we should make love under a dragon
In a four-poster with brass gong rails;
Your toes would be poppy-sleep vermilion;

Your fingers lacquered sagest green. Nightingales
Of gold and lapis lazuli whose song
Might soothe dying emperors would tell

Our lyric love new through all seasons.
But instead I build paper halls
While music drops its scales, reeling

Cathay and Tartary in fluted scrolls
On the air: a princess and prince unknown
Impersonate us, save us their toils

While outside leaves transpare to gold, beaten
By sun and another year's first cold.
I take all this to tell you it is autumn

2. Fable

And when the princess was sick
The beggarman who was of course
A prince in disguise (or was it
The other way round?) came

And lay down across her threshold
Where she slept in silk
So that his heart might keep beating
For both of them if hers should stop
And their breath come and go together.
'You are an extremist,' they said.
To which he answered,
'Our lives are too short for anything less.'

Then you awoke with the fever gone
And I lifted my snout from between
Teardamp paws (your dog, highness),
Rushing at you with nuzzle of kisses
And this paper of old news
That headlines my love.

3. Willow Pattern Plate

I was brought up on Woolworth's willow pattern.
Slices of bread and sugar hid
The blue and white characters.
As you consumed their sweet pap
(Remember grit of granulated crystals
Between the teeth?)
You laid love bare.
I knew it was love
Because of the bluebirds
Skylarking with a ribbon
Up above the bridge
And the lovers were easy to decipher
Under the crumbs and candied flaws.
But the three old men were don'ts,
Strictures: Not-too-much, Not-too-often,
Not-for-ever; the last slice revealed
A whole round puzzle
That no one could explain.
Early you see I was hooked
On love and sweetness,
Ruining my teeth and me together

On a threepenny and sixpenny promise,
Conditioned to expect the two in one,
Though I never found them before,
Only now as we hurry towards each other
I understand that Chinese puzzle:
The old men are ugly and liars
Who can't stop us meeting
On that bridge over the river's laughter
And your love is sweetness on my tongue.

4. Small Pieces of Jade

The much lusted after
Face of our national courtesan
Does not stir me, nor her body.
Can it be that I am growing old?
Or have you so spoiled my palate
For other women?
One thing is certain:
Without you I should starve to death.

*

What should I do but stare
At your bedroom window
While the white moon
Stares at me? The light goes out.
Passersby look up curiously
For a moment then away
As I try to disguise my presence
With an appearance of purpose.
It may be I am as pale
As that moon.

*

You have been gone four years.
So it is though a lying clock
Would say four hours. Tell me

You who tick off my heartbeats
As seconds, who cause seasons
To change in your face,
Who hold me unflickering light years
With those lodestars your eyes
Or draw my tides
With your bellying moon
How is it, mistress of my time,
Our together runs, runs?

*

If I were the little gold fish
We bought today, articulated,
I would swim up the soft canal
Of your body and plash and play
In the deep of you.
Instead, articulate, I send
Shoals of minnow rhymes
To spawn in your head.

5. Drinking Song

Wine is only good when you are not
In love. I have poured in my time
Libations enough, troubling the cots
Of the dead with my hiccups on life.

Across the street they are plucking strings
While I settle the arm of the squat black
Telephone toad on its haunches. It sings
No more with her notes. Throw it back

To sink in a witch's ooze till she
Call me again. Useless the crimson
Cup, perfume of the cassia tree,
Silk screens and hands to beckon me in.

Wine is only good without love,
Without yearning that will vinegar it fast.
Let me lie drunk there, my mouth not move
From the goblet of her white jade breast.

6. Old Age

I find nothing but regret in the sages:
Rahaku in exile,
Po Chü-i recalling a lost daughter;
Threnodies on youth and exhortations
To patience without conviction;
Laments for the unstrung bow,
The failed strength of bowmen;
Girls bathing, green flesh
Under a shower of scooped pearls
Over naked shoulder and breast
While the boys, young warriors,
Curvet out of the bushes.
Age brought them only the delicious
Pain of remembering: 'Time has taken...
And comes no more Spring,
The snows melting, the girl and glass
We shared.'

Sages you have nothing to tell me;
My regrets aren't yours;
Only that I have not loved her
Half a lifetime, that Spring
Passed in a hide and seek where I hunted
Always in the dark. Perhaps it served
The heart's apprenticeship; I was
Being made worthy, mastering
This fine art, firm and delicate
As brushwork, to pleasure her.
Read me no more dry tales of pale youth,
Thwarted ambition, lost places.
Now in my second childhood
She is all countries I would wish to see,
All aspirations and our desire
Passion fruit eaten out of the tin
With a spoon.

☯ Nocturnal for the Winter Solstice

Yesterday, Lucy's forever now,
Shortest though old style your calendar
   Gave a different figure
   Primed with ill luck black enough,
      You might well have thought,
For perpetual mourning, I forgot,
I confess, your obsequies. Unsought
By my usual pilgrim and limping feet,
Grave divine, I offer you this chaplet.

Many times if it had not been for you,
Sir, there in your shroud I couldn't have gone on.
   Your death and hers (whichever one
   Of your gleaming mistresses so
      The object of my worship,
By your proxy favour gone in to trip
A three hundred-year-old measure I slipped
My, your hand to in valediction)
Gave me possibility to live on.

Always at this dropsical season,
Swollen for a nativity not mine
   Like the laid bare belly of an
   Old queen, glutted on faith not reason,
      That lank dogend of a day
Stood me at your elbow, my wreath awry,
Rigid as your marble bones in fancy;
Become stoic in a despair that then
Could not, unliving, die with you again.

I have been your chantry, rehearsed psalms
For your undying lines. Now I must go.
   Give me my indenture. Below
   My neighbours spit on their palms
     For luck and strife but I
Am made in her perpetuity
Master of love who have sought, taught by thee,
Baroque puritan, an aesthetic
Manifest at last in her white fleshed spirit.

Watch with me this little death, this night,
Our wake. Tomorrow my sun renews.
   I have been long, love knows,
   Affected by dreams of saints:
     Magdalen, Thérèse,
Mary, pursued mirages that cease
In her who is all my desert's oasis.
You will forgive me begun so late
That now I only keep time for her days.

Last eve, I boast, I made vigil on her shrine,
Prostrate in our devotions without thought
   Of any death except ours bought
   With our antiphony of crying;
     A death for a death.
You will not be unsung but my breath
Grows shorter and is spent in kisses not grief.
Deep in the solstice of our love we forgot,
I hear you applaud, yours and the world's midnight.

☯ A Baked Potato

Something to take away. Nightshift then:
Going off with my bag of snap to drop
Down the long shaft of evening to the black seams
Of sleep where all night I hack out dreams,
Jet gems, fossils, dead things and, lucky sometimes,
A vein of fool's gold, a glint of you,
With one eye always on the little bird,
Your heart, I carry in my ribcage,
Lest it fall dead and me too.

Oh let no one creep into my bed, your flesh,
While I toil away (no sweated sweet labour
Such as I mine in you); that bird
Trill to me with your remembered tongue.
My own fears poison the air. I hold
Your put-up love warm in my hands
For luck and comfort as the cage goes down.

☯ Mal or I

If I loved you less than
Tristram Iseult
This edge of separation
Might lie blunt
Between us.

Yesterday we hurt ourselves
Unable to make love we opened
The pains in our wrists
And let out the mounting blood
Today we are very gentle
With each other and with the fragile shoots
That have sprung where
We splashed the snow with our cries

I am sunk oh so well deep
In love with you
That I think the stars may go out
For good if I lose again
Even for a syllable's harshness
The Eden tree that grows out
Of our eyes with its golden fruit

May we soon lay the milky comfort
Of our joined flesh over our hunger

Eureka

Turning to sponge a flank
In the bath, a new manoeuvre
Out of laziness, flue, old age,
I discover a big brown mole
That you must often have met
And wonder what else you know
Of me secret from even myself,
What other blemishes of mind
Or body you caress lovingly
Behind my back.

⊗ A Pop Up Card

Tomorrow morning birds and their mates
Will go valentining up the King's Road
In Spring feather.

I sit here trying to carve you
Entwined love knots, initials,
Would paste on my heart
But I cut it out long ago
To hang round your neck.
So there is only a verse
And a love now
As old fangled as our trinity
Or lace cunningly worked
Of sighs, desires, those love knots again,
En bon point on our pillow.
Let them seem fresh to you:
Matter for new marvel.

The dictionary tells me
There were two saints
For this date; martyrs.
They never spilled more heart's blood
Than I would to make you
Red roses out of winter's aconite.

So when you must choose, my turtle,
 And the year awake,
Let me bill and build for you.
Ruffle your plumage white dove;
With you my summer sets on.

Waiting on love the queen
leans to her ministering women
or swings airily
while the black and blue passion clouds
blossom like lovers' pinches.

'During thunder, lightning, rain
are women easily subjected
and in Spring'
I would add snow Kalyana
when both heart and flesh
swoon whitely melting
as today.

Waiting on love I flex
thews, thighs like a dancer
or boxer knowing
I will get as good as I give
have no need of a flowery mantra.

'That which is soft inside
as the filaments of the lotus flower
that is the best'
O Kalyana how could you know
who have not visited her
petalled chamber?

And the women of Guzerat
Larice, Audh, the
Coromandel country, even of
Krishna's own Mathra
with all their amorous virtues
are sluts, whores, baggages unversed
beside her.

Take your recipes of tamarind
quick silver, aniseed of gobstoppers
white panic, brute borax
and pound them into the dust
one touch of her Kalyana would make
your dead bones start
and she is all mine.

Waiting already on our next loving I
rehearse gestures, postures
of our pleasure ornate
with love's invention
our handbook Kalyana
is to lie down together.

Sometimes I am nigh you poor Clare
who were Wellington with his head shot off,
brained Nelson, Lord Juan Byron,
Bard, bruiser Spring fists doubled
against all comers,
cocky bantam in your five foot two
who should have known no more
of rhyme than chants to scare the birds,
vowed to that 'hope, love, joy',
forgetting man can't live by word alone
without bread's wholemeal crumbling on the tongue;
crazed by three witches:
the vampire muse, Mary that never was
from a boy's blush to her old maid death
and that jilt fame who kept you
for a night so you'd remember
then slammed the door at your back.

Sometimes I see you half rimed
from lying out while starlight
slugged you with frost and goblins gabbled
in the park you dared not pass
or porticoed with age under a white thatch
with an obstinate body that couldn't break
or be broken by madhouse bars
and your mind part dark, part gleaming
numbed with the night's cold
as if sent to Maxey for flour
you were faeried off the track forever
and dwell now at the twilight edge
of things, beckoning
Jack o' lantern to lovers, poets.

Yet I can't suck as you did
laudanum at Nature's promiscuous breast,
cornucopian with flowers, beespit, birdhymn
all small sharp sweets;
only her love eases me when I lie down
with the ghoul gab twittering
in my head of loss; the manmade substance
of her pink tissue in my hand
like a crumpled roseleaf
and her perfume phialed, heavy
with echo of her body's musk
charm me against marshlights
your cloudy halfmoon.

Held in her eyes I am.

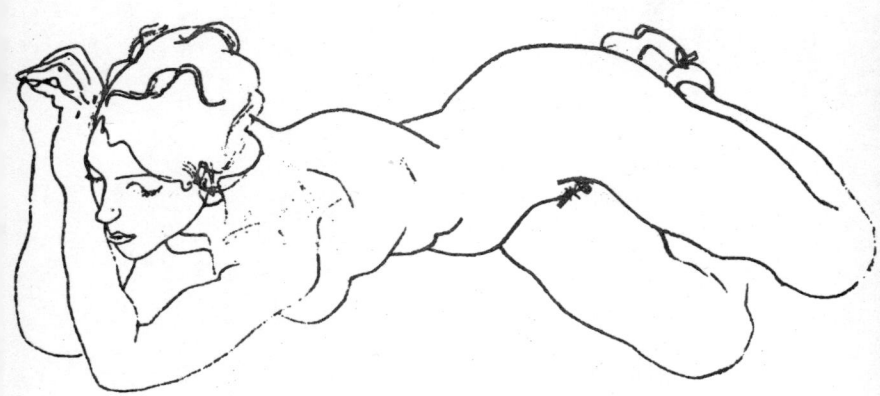